Advent
Together

THE **FAMILY** DEVOTIONAL

Advent Together

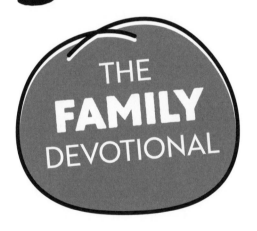

THE **FAMILY** DEVOTIONAL

CWR

STEVE AND BEKAH LEGG

Introduction

It's almost Christmas! We're not quite there yet, but the excitement is beginning to build in our house. We have lots of lovely things that we do every year to help us get ready for Christmas Day. There's a cake to bake, decorations to hang and presents to buy. We love to play Christmas music and have lots of evenings in playing games. It's one of our favourite times of year. A time for family and friends.

In the midst of the tinsel, carols and excitement, it can be easy to forget the reason we celebrate at all. That's why we've written this *Advent Together* book, to help you to put Jesus right back at the centre of Christmas, where He belongs. Whether you read and chat about the daily notes at bedtime, breakfast time or dinner time, we hope this book will help you think about Christmas with fresh eyes. Together you will go on a bit of a journey through the Bible, looking at the plan God had to save the world through Jesus right from the beginning. When we read just one part of the Bible at a time, we might not realise how they all fit together. But all the stories in the Bible are part of God's big story: the story of how much He loves the world and always had a plan to rescue us from the mess we make.

Each day we'll look at a different part of the big story and see the clues that point to the rescue plan, to Jesus. If you look hard enough, you can start finding them all over the place! Steve has put in some of his amazing facts about Christmas in the 'Christmas unwrapped' sections, and we both share some thoughts on the Bible readings.

There's also a section called the 'Jesse tree'. This is a really old tradition from medieval times used to help tell the story of the Bible from creation right through to the life of Jesus. The name comes from Jesse, King David's father. Years before Jesus was born, the prophet Isaiah passed on a message to God's people that God would send a Saviour who would be in Jesse's family tree (Isa. 11:1). Jesus is that Saviour.

Originally, a Jesse tree might have been depicted on a tapestry or a stained glass window to help people who couldn't read to remember God's stories. Nowadays people use the Jesse tree idea a little bit like an Advent calendar, each day hanging an ornament or a picture on a tree to help them remember the Bible stories that point to Jesus.

We thought you might like have a go at making your own Jesse tree! You could put a branch in a vase, make a banner with a tree on it or even use your Christmas tree. Each day, as you read new stories, you'll find some pictures you can trace onto a separate piece of paper or use as inspiration for your own drawing. You can then cut out your drawing and hang it as an ornament on your Jesse tree.

Advent officially starts on the fourth Sunday before Christmas, but we recommend that you start this book on 1 December and finish on Christmas Eve. People aren't sure when Advent was first celebrated, although we do know that some monks were ordered to fast in the weeks up to Christmas in AD 567. That's a long time ago. We don't suggest you do that but we really do hope this book helps you to think and prepare yourself for a Christmas that is focused on Jesus.

Advent means 'coming' in Latin. Jesus came 2,000 years ago. He wants to come into your life, if you'll let Him. And one day, He will come again to rule the world. Our prayer for you over the next few weeks is that as a family you will grow closer together, discovering new things about each other as you meet with Jesus and deepen your relationship with God. We pray that you will know God's presence with you every day, and that this Advent you will be amazed all over again at how the God of the universe came to earth to save you.

Bekah

A new branch

Isaiah 11:1–5

'The royal line of David is like a tree that has been cut down; but just as new branches sprout from a stump, so a new king will arise from among David's descendants.

The Spirit of the LORD will give him wisdom,
and the knowledge and skill to rule his people.
He will know the LORD's will and honour him,
and find pleasure in obeying him.
He will not judge by appearance or hearsay;
he will judge the poor fairly and defend the rights
of the helpless.
At his command the people will be punished,
and evil persons will die.
He will rule his people with justice and integrity.'

Something to think about

God's people had been having a tough time. They hadn't been following His laws for life and they hadn't been taking care of people who needed extra love: children with no parents, old people with no family, or strangers with no home. God had had enough of their behaviour and said He was going to stop it and cut it off, just like you might cut down a big tree to stop it growing. Later on, God's people ended up being taken over by their enemies and living in a foreign land. It felt like the end of the world. But, even though God was tough on their bad behaviour, He always had a plan for hope.

Pointing to Jesus

Today's Bible verses are a message God sent to His people to promise that a new branch would grow out of the stump of the cut-down tree. This new shoot would bring new life and a better way of living for God's people. The branch is Jesus, growing from the stump of His family line that starts with Jesse, the father of King David. There is always hope in Jesus.

Bekah says...

I used to live in Kenya and in the middle of the dry season we sometimes had bush fires. They could be pretty frightening. I lived next to a majestic mountain called Mount Longonot – a luscious, green, extinct volcano. One year, a fire started and the flames grew and covered the mountain. We stayed safe, but my beautiful mountain had turned black. It looked as though everything had died. That was until a few weeks later, when the first few drops of the rainy season fell; green shoots started to appear among the charred remains. It was a beautiful sign that even when it looks like everything is finished, God can bring new life.

Christmas unwrapped

Trees are a very big part of Christmas traditions. People decorate them in all sorts of ways. Martin Luther may have been the first to put lights on a Christmas tree. The story goes that he was out walking one night and the sight of hundreds of stars in the clear night sky moved him to fix candles to the branches of his tree, representing Jesus as the light of the world.

Something to talk about

- Have you ever been through a difficult time, such as lockdown, illness or the death of someone you loved, when everything seemed hopeless?
- How did you find hope?

Pray

God, You always give us hope. Thank You for giving us Jesus. Help us to focus on Him this Advent as we start looking forward to Christmas. Amen.

Jesse tree

We are going to use the idea of a Jesse tree to help us think about how the stories of the Bible point towards Jesus. Today let's hang a picture of a tree stump with a little branch coming out, to help us remember God's promise that even when there is death, He can bring new life.

Trace, cut and colour

DAY 2

Watching and waiting

Habakkuk 2:1–4

'I will climb my watchtower and wait to see what the LORD will tell me to say and what answer he will give to my complaint.

The LORD gave me this answer: "Write down clearly on clay tablets what I reveal to you, so that it can be read at a glance. Put it in writing, because it is not yet time for it to come true. But the time is coming quickly, and what I show you will come true. It may seem slow in coming, but wait for it; it will certainly take place, and it will not be delayed. And this is the message: 'Those who are evil will not survive, but those who are righteous will live because they are faithful to God.'"'

Something to think about

Habakkuk was another of God's prophets passing on messages to God's people. As we meet him today, he has just been having a huge moan at God about how horrible life is for His people and how terrible everyone is being. Habakkuk marches up a big tower to wait and see if God will explain what is going on and what He's going to do about it.

God does answer, but some of His answer is that Habakkuk and the rest of the people need to be patient. God promises that the day will come when He will make the world right and He will stop people from doing terrible things, but they will have to wait and keep watch for that rescue. God asks Habakkuk to make sure he writes the message down so that everyone can see it and have hope that God will make things right.

Pointing to Jesus

God's plan to rescue the world was Jesus. God tells Habakkuk that the time is coming quickly, but it was going to be hundreds of years before Jesus was born. God's sense of time and our sense of time are very different!

Bekah says...

Advent is a time of waiting for Jesus to arrive. Habakkuk was prepared to wait for God to show up, and God's people waited for centuries for their Saviour. We don't have to wait for Jesus any more, but during Advent it's good to keep our eyes focused on Him. We're not just waiting for a special day or presents; we're remembering that God gave the world the best present ever – His Son. And like Habakkuk, our job is to make sure everyone else knows.

Christmas unwrapped

When Jesus did arrive, it wasn't quite how people were expecting. Modern Bethlehem is a bustling town, but at the time of Jesus' birth it was a small, insignificant village, six miles south of Jerusalem. Because of the census, Bethlehem was packed with people registering. All the hotels were full. 'No Vacancy' signs were everywhere. The only place available was a landlord's animal shelter, which meant Jesus ended up coming into the world in a stable. No central heating, clean sheets or antibiotics – and not a midwife in sight. There wasn't even a bed. Instead the tiny new-born baby Jesus was wrapped in a blanket and laid in an animal feeding trough – a manger.

Something to talk about

- What event, big or little, are you waiting for?
- Why is it sometimes hard to wait?

Pray

Father God, waiting is so hard sometimes, because we want to see everything fixed straight away. Help us to be patient and to trust You to mend the world in Your own time. Amen.

Jesse tree

Today we're hanging a picture of a tower on the Jesse tree to remind us that when we are going through hard times, we can talk to God about them and He will answer us just like He did with Habakkuk.

Trace, cut and colour

DAY 3

Family likeness

Genesis 1:26–31

'Then God said, "And now we will make human beings; they will be like us and resemble us. They will have power over the fish, the birds, and all animals, domestic and wild, large and small." So God created human beings, making them to be like himself. He created them male and female, blessed them, and said, "Have many children, so that your descendants will live all over the earth and bring it under their control. I am putting you in charge of the fish, the birds, and all the wild animals. I have provided all kinds of grain and all kinds of fruit for you to eat; but for all the wild animals and for all the birds I have provided grass and leafy plants for food" — and it was done. God looked at everything he had made, and he was very pleased. Evening passed and morning came — that was the sixth day.'

Something to think about

When we think about Jesus, we often think about Him as a baby in a manger. Or we might think of Him grown up and walking on earth. We often forget He existed with God in heaven long before the world began, that He was there at the creation of the universe and everything in it.

This passage reminds us that God made humans to be like Him. He made all kinds of things – mountains and rivers, oceans and great plains. He made amazing animals – great blue whales, tiny little mice and big hairy gorillas. But none of them look like Him in the way that we do. And when God had finished, He was pleased with what He'd made.

Pointing to Jesus

When Jesus was born, He was completely human, *and* completely God. It's confusing and mind-blowing, but it means that Jesus helps us to see what God is like.

Bekah says...

Steve and I have five girls between us. Each of them has something that looks like one of their parents. One has the same eyes and smile as Steve, one has cheeks just like mine, one has the same sense of humour as Steve and one loves explaining things so others understand them, which is just like me.

I love to think that in the same way I have things that are just like my heavenly Father. They might not be my smile or my nose, but they are the kindness I have and the love that I show. They might even include my love for helping people to understand things.

Christmas unwrapped

We all love to sing carols at Christmas, but did you know that when the first Christmas carols were sung, they had a very clear likeness to some well-known tunes of the time? Carols evolved in England way back during the medieval period, and the earliest known carols date from the fifteenth century. They were written in the language of that time and were immediately recognisable by everyone because the melodies mostly came from feasting and folk songs.

Something to talk about

- What aspects of your personality do you think you share with Jesus?
- What physical features and personality traits do you have in common with other members of your family?

Pray

Jesus, thank You for coming that first Christmas to show us what God looks like. Help us to become more like You. Amen.

Jesse tree

Today we're going to hang a picture of Adam and Eve to remind us that we are made in the image of God, and that Jesus has been part of the story of humankind since the beginning.

Trace, cut and colour

Three trees

Genesis 3:6–7,22–23

'The woman saw how beautiful the tree was and how good its fruit would be to eat, and she thought how wonderful it would be to become wise. So she took some of the fruit and ate it. Then she gave some to her husband, and he also ate it. As soon as they had eaten it, they were given understanding and realised that they were naked; so they sewed fig leaves together and covered themselves...

Then the LORD God said, "Now the man has become like one of us and has knowledge of what is good and what is bad. He must not be allowed to take fruit from the tree that gives life, eat it, and live for ever." So the LORD God sent them out of the Garden of Eden and made them cultivate the soil from which they had been formed.'

Something to think about

This is one of the saddest stories in the Bible. God had created the most wonderful world for us to live in. Birds sang, the sun shone and flowers bloomed. It was a place where God and humans could live together. There was just one rule: don't eat the fruit of the tree in the middle of the garden.

Adam and Eve decided not to trust God and they ate the fruit. Because of that, He couldn't trust them to live in His garden anymore and sent them away. Ever since, people haven't been able to live with God in quite the same, perfect way that Adam and Eve had been able to enjoy.

But God had a plan to change everything. The Bible tells us about a new city God is building with another tree in the middle (Rev. 22:2) where His people can live together with Him once again.

Pointing to Jesus

There is another tree that makes it possible for us to be with God again. A tree that got chopped down and made into a cross. A cross that Jesus was nailed to when He took the punishment for the wrong things we have done. Jesus died and rose again so that we could all live with Him.

Bekah says...

Sometimes I say things that I know God wouldn't like. I do things He wouldn't do. And it makes me feel distant from Him. But the amazing thing with God is that He never leaves us, and if we talk to Him and say sorry He always forgives us.

Christmas unwrapped

It happens as November turns to December year in, year out. The tree comes out and the decorations go up. Tatty old cardboard boxes containing tinsel, baubles, lights, candles and nativity figures appear from cupboards, garages and lofts. Some people even go foraging in the country, stripping hedgerows of holly, mistletoe and ivy to decorate homes in festive style. People first started the Christmas tradition of hanging decorations on a tree in sixteenth-century Germany.

Something to talk about

- How can you help one another to stop doing unhelpful and unkind things?
- What do you think would be amazing about living with God?

Pray

Jesus, I'm sorry for messing up sometimes. Thank You for paying the price for me on the cross. Thank You for making it possible for me to know You. I'm excited about living with You one day in heaven. Amen.

Jesse tree

Today we're going to draw a picture of an apple to hang on our Jesse tree to remind us of today's story.

Trace, cut and colour

DAY 5

Are we nearly there yet?

Genesis 12:1–7

'The LORD said to Abram, "Leave your country, your relatives, and your father's home, and go to a land that I am going to show you. I will give you many descendants, and they will become a great nation. I will bless you and make your name famous, so that you will be a blessing.

I will bless those who bless you,

But I will curse those who curse you.

And through you I will bless all the nations."

When Abram was 75 years old, he started out from Haran, as the LORD had told him to do; and Lot went with him. Abram took his wife Sarai, his nephew Lot, and all the wealth and all the slaves they had acquired in Haran, and they started out for the land of Canaan.

When they arrived in Canaan, Abram travelled through the land until he came to the sacred tree of Moreh, the holy place at Shechem. (At that time the Canaanites were still living in the land.) The LORD appeared to Abram and said to him, "This is the country that I am going to give to your descendants." Then Abram built an altar there to the LORD, who had appeared to him.'

Something to think about

Moving house is pretty hard work. All that packing and sorting and lifting is exhausting. But the hard work is usually worth it, and often means a new home and new beginnings. God called Abram and Sarai to leave everything they knew behind and follow Him to a place that He had in mind for them – a place where He would bless them and all their family. Abram and Sarai were pretty old when all this happened, but they trusted God, packed up and set off. God never let them down.

Pointing to Jesus

Jesus went on an even bigger journey. He lived in heaven with God – comfortable, safe and at home. Still, He left all that to come and be born as a baby in a smelly old stable in a dangerous world. He made that journey so that He could show the world just how much God loves them.

Bekah says...

I will never forget moving to Kenya. It was the furthest I'd ever been and although it had seemed like an exciting idea to begin with, when the time came I was pretty frightened. I couldn't take much with me and I didn't know anyone. But God was with me every step of the way. We can never leave Him behind.

Christmas unwrapped

In western Christian tradition, 6 January is known as Epiphany. In some places in Europe, it is also known as Three Kings Day. The actual word 'epiphany' means 'to show' or 'to make known' or even 'to reveal'. Epiphany marks the coming of the wise men who, by bringing gifts, 'revealed' Jesus to the world as Lord and King and the Saviour of all mankind. It was certainly quite a journey – the Magi might have began their travel from an area in Mesopotamia, 700 miles away!

Something to talk about

· When have you had to go somewhere new?
· How did that make you feel?

Pray

Jesus, thank You so much for coming to earth and revealing Your love. Help me to be ready to do big things to help other people know Your love too.
Amen.

Jesse tree

Today we're hanging a picture of a camel and a tent on the tree to show the long journey Abram and Sarai made, and to remind us that Jesus left everything behind for us.

Trace, cut and colour

DAY 6

Stars in the sky

Genesis 15:1–6

'After this, Abram had a vision and heard the LORD say to him, "Do not be afraid, Abram. I will shield you from danger and give you a great reward."

But Abram answered, "Sovereign LORD, what good will your reward do me, since I have no children? My only heir is Eliezer of Damascus. You have given me no children, and one of my slaves will inherit my property."

Then he heard the LORD speaking to him again: "This slave Eliezer will not inherit your property; your own son will be your heir." The LORD took him outside and said, "Look at the sky and try to count the stars; you will have as many descendants as that."

Abram put his trust in the LORD, and because of this the LORD was pleased with him and accepted him.'

Something to think about

Abram loved and trusted God, and God made him the most amazing promise. Abram and Sarai had never been able to have a baby, and they were getting quite old now, but God promised Abram that he would have so many descendants he wouldn't be able to count them all – it would be easier to count the stars in the sky than all the people who would be born into Abram's family!

This promise was hard for Abram to understand because it didn't seem to make any sense at all, but he knew that God was mighty and powerful and so he trusted Him anyway. Abram knew God was able to do things he couldn't even imagine.

Pointing to Jesus

Later on, God told Abram that all the world would be blessed through his descendants. Abram's children, grandchildren and great-grandchildren became the Israelites, God's people who showed the world what a great God He is. But even later than that, Jesus came along – and if you trace His family line back far enough, eventually you get to Abram. That really is a blessing.

Bekah says...

How many stars can you see in the sky? Can you imagine a bigger family than that? Abram's family was huge, but now it's even bigger because it includes everyone that follows Jesus. You and I have been adopted into God's family. Being in God's family is wonderful; race, background and education just don't matter as we have our faith in common. It's like we've been grafted onto that Jesse tree. All these stories we read in the lead up to Christmas are about our adopted family – our great, great-grandads and grannies.

Christmas unwrapped

Sport can often bring people together in remarkable ways. On Christmas Day 1914, during the First World War, soldiers from both sides met up in 'No Man's Land' for a very special game of football. For a few hours, enemy met enemy between the trenches in Northern France as a football was produced and a kick-around ensued. Though British and German troops made up the majority of the teams, French and Belgians joined in too for an impromptu game of footie. While friends and loved ones at home were eating their Christmas dinner, soldiers from different sides were playing football, laughing, chatting and shaking hands with the very men they had been trying to kill just a few hours earlier. It was astounding.

Something to talk about

· How big is your family?
· What does it feel like to be part of God's big family?

Pray

God of Abram, thank You for making me part of Your family. Help me to invite others to come and be part of it too. Amen.

Jesse tree

Today we're going to hang a star on the Jesse tree to remind us that God keeps His promises.

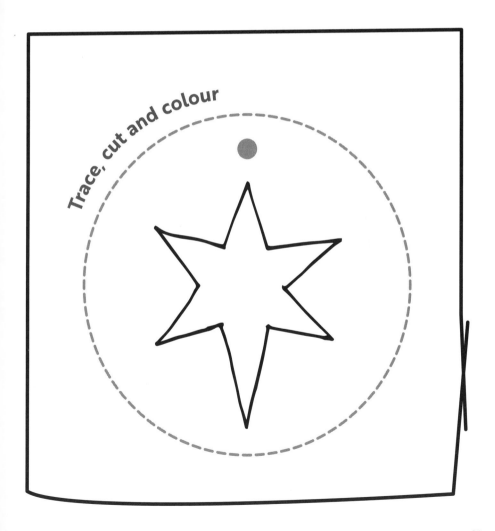

Trace, cut and colour

A big sacrifice

 Genesis 22:1–2,9–13

'Sometime later God tested Abraham; he called to him, "Abraham!" And Abraham answered, "Yes, here I am!"

"Take your son," God said, "your only son, Isaac, whom you love so much, and go to the land of Moriah. There on a mountain that I will show you, offer him as a sacrifice to me."...

When they came to the place which God had told him about, Abraham built an altar and arranged the wood on it. He tied up his son and placed him on the altar, on top of the wood. Then he picked up the knife to kill him. But the angel of the Lord called to him from heaven, "Abraham, Abraham!"

He answered, "Yes, here I am."

"Don't hurt the boy or do anything to him," he said. "Now I know that you honour and obey God, because you have not kept back your only son from him."

Abraham looked around and saw a ram caught in a bush by its horns. He went and got it and offered it as a burnt offering instead of his son.'

Something to think about

Can you imagine how Abraham (Abram, after God changed both his and Sarai's names!) must have felt when God asked him to give up his son? Probably frightened, angry and sad all at the same time. And confused. God had promised more descendants than Abraham could count through this special son, Isaac, who had been born to Abraham and Sarah in their old age. Now God was asking Abraham to sacrifice his only son.

But Abraham also knew that God keeps His promises. So, as he headed up the mountain, he must have been counting on God to make a way to keep His promise. God did exactly that and provided a ram to take Isaac's place.

Pointing to Jesus

Centuries later, God kept His promise to His people again when He provided another lamb as a sacrifice. Just like Abraham, God was prepared to give His precious Son to show how much He loved the world. That Lamb of God was Jesus, the one we're waiting for this Advent.

Bekah says...

I don't have many valuable things; I don't have expensive jewellery or fancy art. The things I most value are the people I love - Steve, our girls, and our friends and family. It's a real challenge to think about putting God first, making Him the most valuable thing in my life. But the fact that He gave His only Son to die for me helps me to understand just how big His love is. It's a pretty special kind of love.

Christmas unwrapped

Those first ever Christmas presents of gold, frankincense and myrrh have probably become the most well-known gifts ever given. As well as being hugely valuable, each gift was loaded with significance and symbolism. Gold was a very precious gift that was usually presented to kings; frankincense was an expensive fragrance that was used in worship; myrrh came from the stems and branches of a prickly shrub and was used to anoint a dead body. Can you see how they were perfect gifts for Jesus?

Something to talk about

- What is the most valuable thing you own?
- Is there anything in the world you'd give it up for?

Pray

Dear Father God, thank You for always keeping Your promises, even when that meant giving up Your most precious thing – Your Son. Thank You for sending Jesus to earth to rescue us. Help us to trust Your promises like Abraham did, and to know that You always make a way. Amen.

Jesse tree

Today we're hanging a sheep on the tree to remind us that God always provides a way for us to follow Him, just like He did for Abraham.

Trace, cut and colour

A special son

Genesis 37:3–5,23–4,28

'Jacob loved Joseph more than all his other sons, because he had been born to him when he was old. He made a long robe with full sleeves for him. When his brothers saw that their father loved Joseph more than he loved them, they hated their brother so much that they would not speak to him in a friendly manner.

One night Joseph had a dream, and when he told his brothers about it, they hated him even more... When Joseph came up to his brothers, they ripped off his long robe with full sleeves. Then they took him and threw him into the well, which was dry... and when some Midianite traders came by, the brothers pulled Joseph out of the well and sold him for twenty pieces of silver to the Ishmaelites, who took him to Egypt.'

Something to think about

Little brothers (and sisters) can be pretty annoying, and Joseph really knew how to wind his brothers up – telling them about his dreams that one day he would be in charge of them all. He was his dad's favourite son and thought he could get away with anything.

He couldn't – big brothers can be pretty bad too, and Joseph wasn't safe with his at all. It wasn't long before his big brothers had had enough of him, took away his special coat, threw him in a well and sold him for 20 pieces of silver.

Pointing to Jesus

Joseph's story isn't the only story in the Bible of someone being betrayed by people who were meant to love him. Jesus was God's special Son and when He came to earth and started telling people who He really was, people didn't like that either. They betrayed Him for 30 pieces of silver and took His coat too.

Bekah says...

I used to argue with my little brother – a lot. My parents never had favourites, I just found him really annoying when he wanted to play with me when my friends were around – and even when I was on my own I found him annoying. But I did love him underneath all my grumpiness, and as we've grown up we've become really good friends. I love to hang out with him nowadays. I even like to ask him for advice when I've got a problem!

Christmas unwrapped

We see holly on cards, in shops and we have it in our homes. Its bright red berries and sturdy, shiny leaves brighten up the darkest, dullest winter days. There have been many strange rituals involving holly over the centuries but it was only when Christians associated holly with the death of Jesus (the leaves representing the crown of thorns pushed on His head, and the berries the red drops of blood that He shed) that it officially became part of the Christmas celebrations we know today.

Something to talk about

· What do you do that winds up your family members?
· What could you do to be kind to them?

Pray

Dear Lord Jesus, we're sorry for the times we're like Joseph and we show off. We're sorry for the times we're like Joseph's brothers and we're not patient and hurt people we're meant to love. Thank You that You know what it feels like to be let down and that You're always with us, even when it feels like we're all alone. Amen.

Jesse tree

Today we're going to hang multi-coloured coat – just like Joseph's – on our tree to remind us that Jesus knows what it's like to be hurt by friends and to love them anyway.

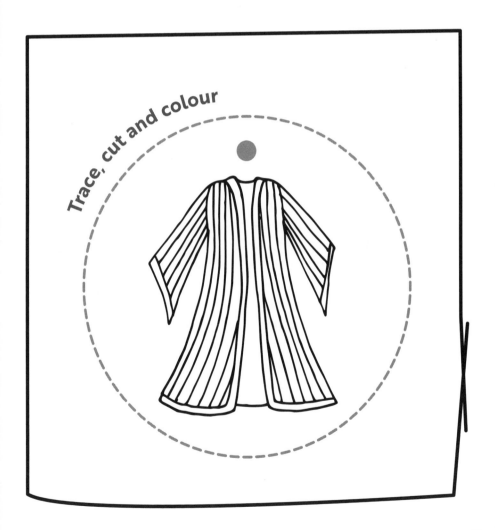

Trace, cut and colour

DAY 9

Red rope

Joshua 2:1–3,8–9,13–14,18

'Then Joshua sent two spies from the camp at Acacia with orders to go and secretly explore the land of Canaan, especially the city of Jericho. When they came to the city, they went to spend the night in the house of... Rahab. The king of Jericho heard that some Israelites had come that night to spy out the country, so he sent word to Rahab: "The men in your house have come to spy out the whole country! Bring them out!"...

Rahab went up on the roof and said [to the spies], "I know that the LORD has given you this land. Everyone in the country is terrified of you... Promise me that you will save my father and mother, my brothers and sisters, and all their families! Don't let us be killed!"

The men said to her, "May God take our lives if we don't do as we say! If you do not tell anyone what we have been doing, we promise you that when the LORD gives us this land, we will treat you well."...

"This is what you must do. When we invade your land, tie this red cord to the window you let us down from."'

Something to think about

Jesus' family tree is full of some unexpected people – and perhaps the most unexpected person is Rahab. She wasn't even an Israelite, one of God's people. Not at first, anyway. But when two Israelite spies came to check out the city of Jericho, she took them in and protected them. She believed in their God and asked for protection when the Israelite army come to knock down Jericho.

The spies agreed to save her, and they told her to hang a red rope from her window so that they knew which house to look out for. When the time came, Rahab and her family were saved.

Pointing to Jesus

That red rope might have looked a bit like a trail of blood, which reminds us of the blood of Jesus. Centuries later, Rahab's very-great-grandson died on the cross to save our lives, just like her red cord saved her life. If we trust in God, like Rahab, we can join His family too.

Bekah says...

Some of my happiest moments have been when our girls have made the decision to trust God. They were always part of our Legg family, but now we are all part of God's family – together. It really matters that we make our own decision to trust God and follow Him. Other people can't decide for us.

Christmas unwrapped

The rope showed Rahab to be a friend of Israel and now even a family member. One of the ways we show our friends and family how much we care about them at Christmas is by sending cards. John Callcott Horsley was a well-known painter who designed the first Christmas card in December 1843 at the request of his friend, Sir Henry Cole, the founding director of the Victoria and Albert Museum. The custom of sending cards took a good few years to properly take off. But take off it did. Around one billion cards are sent each year in the UK!

Something to talk about

· If you love Jesus, when did you decide to be part of God's family?
· What helped you make that decision?

Pray

Jesus, thank You for being prepared to die for me, so that I could live forever with You. Thank You that anyone and everyone can be part of Your family. Thank You for loving me. Amen.

Jesse tree

Today, let's hang a red rope or ribbon on the Jesse tree to remind us that God protects and rescues us.

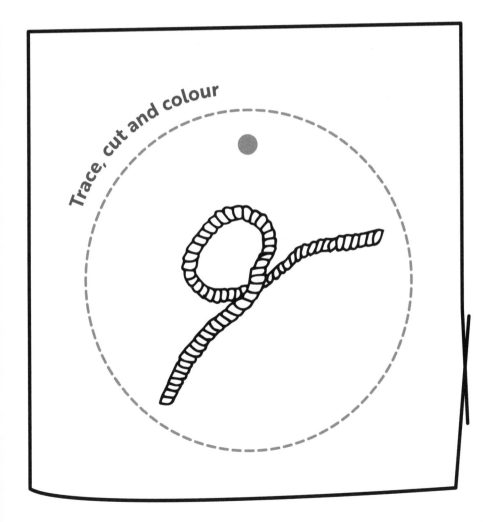

Trace, cut and colour

Hero to the rescue

Ruth 3:1–5

'So Ruth gleaned in the field until evening. Then she threshed the barley she had gathered, and it amounted to about an ephah. She carried it back to town, and her mother-in-law saw how much she had gathered. Ruth also brought out and gave her what she had left over after she had eaten enough.

Her mother-in-law asked her, "Where did you glean today? Where did you work? Blessed be the man who took notice of you!"

Then Ruth told her mother-in-law about the one at whose place she had been working. "The name of the man I worked with today is Boaz," she said.

"The Lord bless him!" Naomi said to her daughter-in-law. "He has not stopped showing his kindness to the living and the dead." She added, "That man is our close relative; he is one of our guardian-redeemers."

Then Ruth the Moabite said, "He even said to me, 'Stay with my workers until they finish harvesting all my grain.'"'

Something to think about

Thousands of years ago, when this story happened, women didn't have much power. If their husband died and they didn't have sons then they were all alone in the world with no one to look after them. Tragically, they would often end up desperately poor and hungry. This is what had happened to Ruth and Naomi.

God gave rules stating that the nearest relative should take care of a widow and her family. Boaz was especially kind because he wasn't the nearest relative, but he chose to look after Ruth and Naomi anyway. He understood that God's laws were about loving those who were really struggling, not just keeping the rules.

Pointing to Jesus

Later in the story, Boaz married Ruth and they became part of Jesus' family tree too. Years later Jesus would come along and do the same thing Boaz did – but for the whole world. He stepped in, even though He didn't have to, and provided everything we need. The Bible even says that we are like Jesus' bride.

Bekah says...

When Steve and I got married we brought our two families together. He had three girls and I had two. (What a lot of girls!) We sometimes talk about when we all got married, even though it was only Steve and I who made promises to each other. But ever since that day we've all been one family, looking out for each other and taking care of each other. Families can all look very different, but they're pretty special.

Christmas unwrapped

Despite how it sounds, Boxing Day – the day after Christmas Day – has nothing to do with having a fight! It seems to have been a British idea and is also known as St Stephen's Day, named after the first Christian martyr. According to tradition, it was a day when aid boxes were opened in churches, with the money given to the poor in the parish. What a great demonstration of God's love for those in need.

Something to talk about

- Have you ever done something kind for someone, even when you didn't have to?
- What made you do that?

Pray

Jesus, thank You for making a way for us to be part of Your family, even when You didn't have to. Thank You for loving us always. Amen.

Jesse tree

Today we're going to hang a sheaf of corn on our Jesse tree. Ruth first went to collect scraps of left-over wheat from Boaz's fields, but he ended up giving her much, much more than he had to. Just like Jesus.

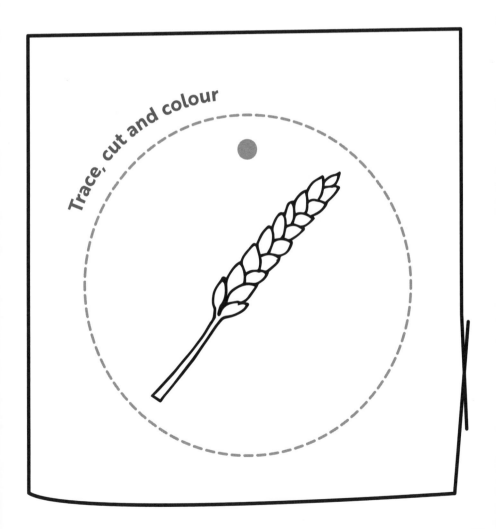

Trace, cut and colour

An unexpected king

1 Samuel 16:1,10–13

'The LORD said to Samuel, "How long will you go on grieving over Saul? I have rejected him as king of Israel. But now get some olive oil and go to Bethlehem, to a man named Jesse, because I have chosen one of his sons to be king."...

Jesse brought seven of his sons to Samuel. And Samuel said to him, "No, the LORD hasn't chosen any of these." Then he asked him, "Do you have any more sons?"

Jesse answered, "There is still the youngest, but he is out taking care of the sheep."

"Tell him to come here," Samuel said. "We won't offer the sacrifice until he comes." So Jesse sent for him. He was a handsome, healthy young man, and his eyes sparkled. The LORD said to Samuel, "This is the one—anoint him!" Samuel took the olive oil and anointed David in front of his brothers. Immediately the spirit of the LORD took control of David and was with him from that day on.'

Something to think about

David was the youngest brother of a not very special family and he was just a shepherd – not a job people wanted to have. Nobody would have expected him to be king. But God had other plans, and David went on to be one of the best kings Israel ever had. When God uses people who couldn't do the job by themselves, it helps people to see how amazing God is because it's obvious that He's the one giving them the ability to do well.

Pointing to Jesus

When Jesus was born, people had been waiting for years for a great hero to come and be their Saviour, to rescue them from their enemies. No one was expecting a baby born in a stable with a couple of nobodies for parents. He wasn't born into a royal family; His dad was just a carpenter. When He grew up He wasn't a great warrior; He let people take Him and kill Him without a fight.

Bekah says...

My friends have started an amazing community centre in our town. Everyone told them it was impossible, but they did it anyway. Someone else said they'd need a big business to give them loads of money, but they said no. Their plan seemed bonkers, but eight months in, God provided just what they needed at just the right time. People have walked in off the street and offered them everything from industrial dishwashers to chandeliers and a team to deep-clean. It's amazing and it shows our whole community that God is awesome.

Christmas unwrapped

The 'three kings' in the Christmas story were actually non-Jewish astronomers and astrologers. There weren't necessarily just three of them either; there could have been more wise men, visiting Jesus with their Christmas presents. When they finally arrived in Bethlehem (perhaps up to two years later) they fell on their knees and worshipped the little boy. These men were great scholars and of a different race, culture and religion than Mary and Joseph. Yet here they were, worshipping their toddler. It must have been quite a sight.

Something to talk about

- Can you think of other Bible stories where God has worked in unexpected ways?
- How would you like God to use you in the world?

Pray

Dear God, thank You that You like to use people that the world doesn't think are important. Please use me too. Amen.

Jesse tree

Today we're going to hang a shepherd's crook on the tree. Shepherds were some of the lowest people around, and this crook will help us remember that God uses the people we least expect in order to do His work.

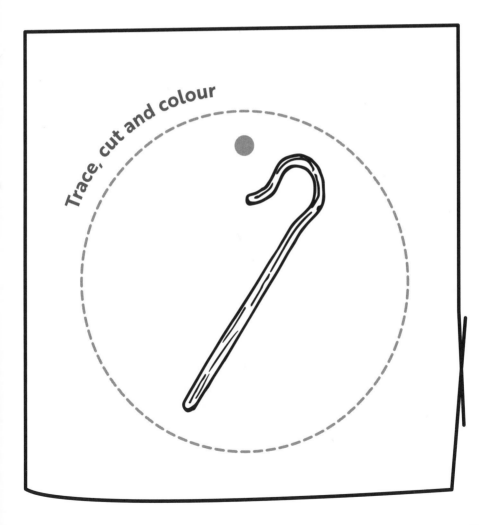

Trace, cut and colour

A shepherd king

2 Samuel 5:1–3

'Then all the tribes of Israel went to David at Hebron and said to him, "We are your own flesh and blood. In the past, even when Saul was still our king, you led the people of Israel in battle, and the LORD promised you that you would lead his people and be their ruler." So all the leaders of Israel came to King David at Hebron. He made a sacred alliance with them, they anointed him, and he became king of Israel.'

Something to think about

Shepherds and kings were at opposite ends of the spectrum. One sat on a throne in expensive clothes, and the other stood in the fields talking to sheep. Everyone respected and admired the king. The shepherds, however, were totally ignored. But David was both. God chose this shepherd to be king of His special people. It makes sense: David was used to taking care of his sheep, protecting them and making sure that they had what they needed – even caring for them before himself. God wanted David to be like that with His people.

Pointing to Jesus

God chose David to be His shepherd king, but one day He gave the world another. Jesus called Himself the good shepherd, willing to die for His sheep (John 10:11). David was an awesome king but he was just a glimpse of who Jesus would be.

Bekah says...

It's easy to think that leading is all about being bossy and giving orders. I'm sure we all know people like that, and we're probably sometimes like it ourselves. God has a different idea of what good leadership is - it's serving others. Jesus even washed His disciples' feet to show them what real leadership looks like. I know some great leaders who have a similar attitude: teachers who work late into the night to prepare for their lessons and who use their own money to buy pens and props for the classroom; medical and emergency service workers who risk their lives to protect the public; youth leaders who give up their free time to take young people on camps that will change their lives.

Christmas unwrapped

In 1847, the Christmas cracker was invented by a baker and confectioner, Tom Smith. He was adventurous and quite an entrepreneur and often travelled abroad to search for new ideas. It was on a trip to Paris in 1840 that he first discover the bonbon, a sugar almond sweet wrapped in a twist of tissue paper. In London, Tom first started to place messages in the wrappings, then he replaced the sweets with gifts. It was the crackle of a log as he threw it on his fire that gave him the final flash of inspiration, which eventually led to the crackers we love to pull these days.

Something to talk about

· Why would a shepherd make such a good king?
· In what ways do you look out for other people?

Pray

King Jesus, thank You for having the heart of a shepherd and laying Your life down for us. We pray for our leaders to have a heart like Yours and always look out for their people. Amen.

Jesse tree

Let's hang a crown on our Jesse tree today to remind us that Jesus is the King of kings but that never stopped Him from giving up everything for us – just like a shepherd.

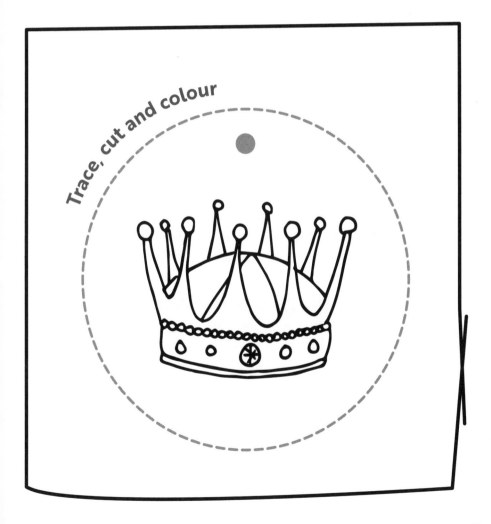

Trace, cut and colour

A Temple

1 Kings 5:5; 6:11–14

'The LORD promised my father David, "Your son, whom I will make king after you, will build a temple for me." And I have now decided to build that temple for the worship of the LORD my God...

The LORD said to Solomon, "If you obey all my laws and commands, I will do for you what I promised your father David. I will live among my people Israel in this Temple that you are building, and I will never abandon them."

So Solomon finished building the Temple.'

Something to think about

The Temple that Solomon built was amazing. If you read the rest of 1 Kings 6 you will see just how magnificent it was – tall, full of gold and covered in intricate carvings on beautiful wood and stone. It was stunning. But it was more than an impressive piece of architecture; more than a clever design carried out by master builders and artists, it was where God lived.

Until the Temple was built, God's people had carried a leather tent everywhere they went. It was a meeting place for God and His people, but this Temple replaced that. Deep inside was a special room called the holy of holies and it was here that priests could encounter God and be in His presence.

Pointing to Jesus

Eventually, Israel's enemies destroyed the Temple. It was rebuilt years later, but God always had a much better plan. He was about to make a way for anyone to be able to be in His presence, anywhere and everywhere. That plan was Jesus. Jesus even called Himself the Temple (John 2:19). We don't have to go into a special room anymore. Jesus was God and man – He is the meeting place. If we know Jesus, we know God.

Bekah says...

I have some places where I feel it's easy to talk to God – I love praying while I walk the dog on the beach. But the truth is God is with me everywhere I go. And I've been to a lot of places. I've sat on the beaches of East Africa, fished in Lake Victoria, flown in a tiny plane to a tiny island off the coast of Haiti and taught children in a village in India. Wherever I go, God is with me because I have Jesus living in me.

Christmas unwrapped

Mince pies were once deemed to be far too fancy and were banned by Oliver Cromwell! (More about him another day.) They had first been made as early as 1390 when they were filled with pork, boiled eggs and cheese before mixing them with spices and seasoning. Not quite how I make them!

Something to talk about

· Do you have somewhere that you feel close to God?
· If you were making a special home for God to live in, what would it look like?

Pray

Jesus, thank You for giving up Your throne in heaven to become human like us. Help us to understand what it really means that You were both God and man. We are so grateful that we can know You and talk with You all the time. Amen.

Jesse tree

Let's hang a picture of a temple on the tree today to remind us that Jesus came to be our temple – the place where we can meet with God.

Trace, cut and colour

Risk

Esther 4:13–17

'"Don't imagine that you are safer than any other Jew just because you are in the royal palace. If you keep quiet at a time like this, help will come from heaven to the Jews, and they will be saved, but you will die and your father's family will come to an end. Yet who knows—maybe it was for a time like this that you were made queen!"

Esther sent Mordecai this reply: "Go and get all the Jews in Susa together; hold a fast and pray for me. Don't eat or drink anything for three days and nights. My servant women and I will be doing the same. After that, I will go to the king, even though it is against the law. If I must die for doing it, I will die."

Mordecai then left and did everything that Esther had told him to do.'

Something to think about

Esther and Mordecai were Jews, living in a foreign land, ruled by a king who didn't know God. Incredibly, Esther had been chosen to be queen, but now she was in a terrible place. Her husband, without realising, had condemned all the Jews in the land to death.

Esther had an enormous choice to make: she could stay quiet and hope no one realised she was a Jew, or she could speak up, go and talk to the king and risk being killed herself. With her Uncle Mordecai's help and prayer, Esther decided to take the risk and try to save her people.

Pointing to Jesus

Esther was willing to die if it meant her people might be saved. Does that remind you of anyone? Jesus was prepared to die too. In fact, He *did* die – to save us and give us life. It didn't end there, though. He rose again and has beaten death once and for all.

Bekah says...

I go skiing with the girls most years, but the truth is, I'm pretty scared of heights. When Megan was just five years old she was having a ski lesson and fell and broke her leg. I was at the top of the mountain and the quickest way to get to her was down a very steep slope that terrified me. Wanting to get to her so she felt safe was more important to me than my fear, so I quickly made it down the scary slope. It's the only time I've managed it!

Christmas unwrapped

Noël is the French word for Christmas. In France, during Christmas time, nearly every home displays a nativity scene or *crèche* filled with small clay figures called *santons* or 'little saints'. As well as the baby Jesus and His parents, shepherds and Magi, there are also little figures in the form of local people in high-ranking positions.

Something to talk about

- Have you ever done something difficult or scary to help someone?
- What made you choose to do that?

Pray

Jesus, You are so brave and so kind. Thank You for being willing to die for me even though I don't really deserve such kindness. Help me to be brave like You and to put myself out for other people so they can see Your love in my actions. Amen.

Jesse tree

Today we're hanging a royal sceptre on the Jesse tree. When Esther went to see the king she had to wait and see if he held out his sceptre towards her. If he did, she would live. If he didn't, she would die. It's a reminder that Jesus, like Esther, was ready to die for His friends on earth.

Trace, cut and colour

DAY 15

A great light

Isaiah 9:2–3,6–7

'The people who walked in darkness
   have seen a great light.
They lived in a land of shadows,
   but now light is shining on them.
You have given them great joy, Lord;
   you have made them happy...
A child is born to us!
   A son is given to us!
   And he will be our ruler.
He will be called, "Wonderful Counsellor,"
   "Mighty God," "Eternal Father,"
   "Prince of Peace."
His royal power will continue to grow;
   his kingdom will always be at peace.'

Something to think about

This is a beautiful bit of the Bible where God's prophet Isaiah reminds the people that God has a plan to bring light into the darkness. God's people were in really dark times. They'd been doing all kinds of things that didn't please God. They'd been captured and taken to another country, and they couldn't see a way out.

Through Isaiah, God was promising that the sun always rises again. That He will bring an end to their suffering and restore His kingdom on the earth.

Pointing to Jesus

These verses are a huge signpost to Jesus. The nativity story tells us all about the 'child... born to us'. Jesus called Himself the light of the world (John 8:12), and this passage gives us some other ideas of who He is: 'Mighty God', 'Prince of Peace', a King.

Bekah says...

When I lived in Africa there weren't a lot of street lights, so it was really dark at night. The amazing thing about that was it meant you could see a lot more stars. Often the moon shone so brightly, you could see pretty well.

Christmas unwrapped

Today's reading hints at Jesus coming that first Christmas and is the reason we celebrate at this time of year. But did you know Oliver Cromwell tried to scrap Christmas? He wanted Christmas returned to a very sombre and religious occasion where people only thought about the birth of Jesus, rather than eating and drinking or celebrating. So in the 1640s he banned Christmas. Special food (including those mince pies they used to eat) and even holly were banned, but thankfully by 1660 the law was thrown out and Jesus' birth could be celebrated again. Christmas was back.

Something to talk about

· How do you feel when it's very dark?
· How do you feel when it's light?

Pray

Father God, thank You for Your promise to bring light into the darkness. Thank You for being the light of our lives. Please help us turn the world's darkness into light. Amen.

Jesse tree

Today we're going to hang a sun on the Jesse tree. Christmas is when we remember that Jesus was the light in the darkness, and Advent is when we get ready to celebrate the arrival of that light.

Trace, cut and colour

Animal kingdom

Isaiah 11:5–8

*'He will rule his people with justice and integrity.
Wolves and sheep will live together in peace,
   and leopards will lie down with young goats.
Calves and lion cubs will feed together,
   and little children will take care of them.
Cows and bears will eat together,
   and their calves and cubs will lie down in peace.
Lions will eat straw as cattle do.
Even a baby will not be harmed
   if it plays near a poisonous snake.'*

Something to think about

Isaiah had more to say about Jesus and the difference
He would make to the world. But today's verses seem a
bit crazy. Wolves and sheep living together without the
wolf eating the sheep, and leopards relaxing with goats
sounds more like the ending of a Disney movie! It's pretty
fantastical. Our world just isn't like that. Cows and bears
don't eat together; the bears would chow down on the
cows. Lions don't snack on straw; they eat meat – other

animals. And it's hard to imagine any parent letting their child take care of lion cubs or play with poisonous snakes either. That would go horribly wrong very quickly.

Pointing to Jesus

Isaiah hasn't lost his mind, he's pointing to a world that will one day be possible because of Jesus. This world where lions and lambs can be friends is like the world God created, before humans broke it. One day God will restore that world and, because of Jesus, we can join Him there in safety – there will be no more fighting or fear. That's something to look forward to!

Bekah says...

When I lived in Africa, my home was next-door to a place called Elsamere. It had once been the home of an amazing lady called Joy Adamson who rescued an orphan lion cub and raised it. The lion was called Elsa and grew up with the family in the house, before she was released back into the wild. Afterwards Joy and her husband raised a cheetah and a leopard too. A film called Born Free was made about her story. I'd have loved to see it for real.

Christmas unwrapped

You don't often see cows and bears together in the wild but you're quite likely to (well, it would be someone dressed up as one) if you visit a pantomime over the Christmas period. It's a comedy play where everyone dresses up in ridiculous costumes, there are shouts of 'he's behind you' and 'oh no he isn't – oh yes he is', accompanied by lots of booing and hissing. The sketchy plots are based loosely on traditional fairy tales. such as Cinderella, Aladdin and Dick Whittington. It's thought that pantomine plays originated in the sixteenth century by travelling players in Italy and France.

Something to talk about

- In a world where animals can be friends, which would you most like to play with?
- What animal do you think you're like, and why?

Pray

Dear God, I am so excited about the day when I can meet all the different animals You have created and not be afraid of them. Thank You, Jesus, for making it possible. Please bring Your kingdom soon. Amen.

Jesse tree

Let's hang a picture of a wolf and a lamb together to remind us of the world Jesus has made possible for us.

Trace, cut and colour

Turn around

Jonah 3:1–8

'Once again the LORD spoke to Jonah. He said, "Go to Nineveh, that great city, and proclaim to the people the message I have given you." So Jonah obeyed the LORD and went to Nineveh, a city so large that it took three days to walk through it. Jonah started through the city, and after walking a whole day, he proclaimed, "In forty days Nineveh will be destroyed!"

The people of Nineveh believed God's message. So they decided that everyone should fast, and all the people, from the greatest to the least, put on sackcloth to show that they had repented.

When the king of Nineveh heard about it, he got up from his throne, took off his robe, put on sackcloth, and sat down in ashes. He sent out a proclamation to the people of Nineveh: "This is an order from the king and his officials... Everyone must pray earnestly to God and must give up their wicked behaviour and their evil actions."'

Something to think about

The story of Jonah is incredible, but not just because he was swallowed by a large fish! It's the fact that the Ninevites, who had been doing such bad things, turned their lives around to follow God when Jonah asked them. The Ninevites were powerful and scary, and Jonah didn't want to risk being the one to tell them they'd upset God. In truth, Jonah didn't like them and wanted them to be punished.

When Jonah gave a massive 'No!' to His plans, God gave Jonah three days in the dark in the stomach of a fish to think about it and turn his own life around so that he could go and give God's message to the city of Ninevah. It's amazing what can happen when we just follow where God leads us.

Pointing to Jesus

Jesus also spent three days in a dark place, but not because He was running away from God. Jesus always did what His Father asked, even when that was scary. Even when it meant dying on a cross. Jesus' obedience meant we can turn our lives around and follow God too, just like the Ninevites.

Bekah says...

Being obedient doesn't always sound like a lot of fun. I certainly don't always like being told what to do, and our girls really don't like it when I ask them to tidy their rooms, be home by a certain time or help out around the house. Learning to listen and obey people who love us is important and it can help us practise listening to God and obeying Him too.

Christmas unwrapped

Every year, Queen Elizabeth II broadcasts a special message on Christmas Day. This tradition dates back to 1932, when her grandfather (King George V) first spoke on the radio to the British Empire. The transmission went out live at 3pm, which was the best time to reach most of the countries. Queen Elizabeth II made her first speech on live radio in 1952, but these days the speeches are pre-recorded.

Something to talk about

· When have you found it hard to do what you've been asked?
· What helps you to follow instructions?

Pray

Dear God, thank You for having a plan to rescue everyone – even people who have done bad things like the Ninevites. I'm so glad I can be part of Your plan. Help me to obey You and show me what I can do today for You. Amen.

Jesse tree

Today we're hanging a picture of a whale to remind us of Jonah's story, and to help us remember to follow God and obey Him so that we can help other people to get to know Him too.

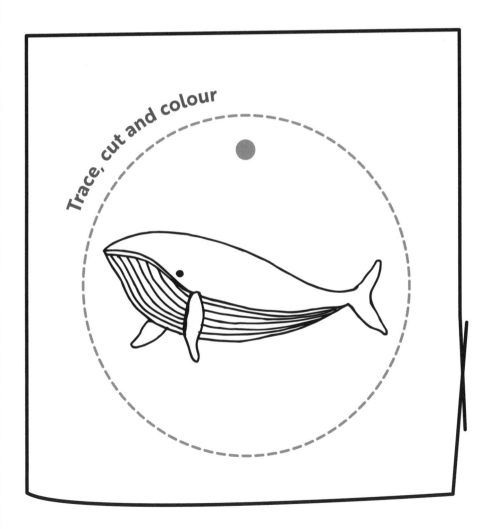

Trace, cut and colour

God is with us

Daniel 6:11–13,16,19–22

'When Daniel's enemies observed him praying to God, all of them went together to the king to accuse Daniel. They said, "Your Majesty, you signed an order that for the next thirty days anyone who requested anything from any god or from any human being except you, would be thrown into a pit filled with lions... Daniel, one of the exiles from Judah... prays regularly three times a day."...

So the king gave orders for Daniel to be taken and thrown into the pit filled with lions...

At dawn the king got up and hurried to the pit. When he got there, he called out anxiously, "Daniel, servant of the living God! Was the God you serve so loyally able to save you from the lions?"

Daniel answered, "May Your Majesty live forever! God sent his angel to shut the mouths of the lions so that they would not hurt me. He did this because he knew that I was innocent and because I have not wronged you, Your Majesty."'

Something to think about

Following God isn't always easy. Sometimes it's downright dangerous. Daniel was following God even though he was in a foreign land, ruled by a foreign king who had passed a rule that meant no one could pray to God. But Daniel knew talking with God was important, so he did it anyway. He stood out from the crowd.

Daniel was able to be brave because he fully believed God was more powerful than the king. And Daniel was right. God sent an angel to be with him in the lions' den, to close their mouths. When God sends an angel, He is sending it as His representative. It was like God was there in the pit with Daniel.

Pointing to Jesus

Centuries later, God sent someone else to be with His people in their difficult times. God was sending His own Son, Jesus, to be with His people.

Bekah says...

Living in Kenya was amazing – but sometimes pretty scary. One night I woke up in a fright; I could hear a noise in my bedroom like heavy breathing, but I knew that no one else was around. I didn't know what to do except pray. Eventually I was brave enough to turn on my light and see what was in the room with me. It was a buffalo sticking its head through my bedroom window! Fortunately, it couldn't get in any further.

Christmas unwrapped

Robert May wrote a story in 1939 about a reindeer who was teased by the other reindeer because of his bright red nose. Robert toyed with calling the reindeer Rollo or Reginald, but the name was finally suggested by the author's young daughter, and Rudolph the Red-Nosed Reindeer was born.

Something to talk about

· When has God made you feel brave?
· What does it feel like to know God's presence with you?

Pray

Jesus, thank You for never leaving us on our own. Thank You for being the powerful Lion of Judah who protects His people. Help me to always look to You when I'm afraid. Amen.

Jesse tree

Hang a lion on your Jesse tree today. It's a reminder that God is with us in the most frightening of times. It's also one of the names of Jesus – the Lion of Judah.

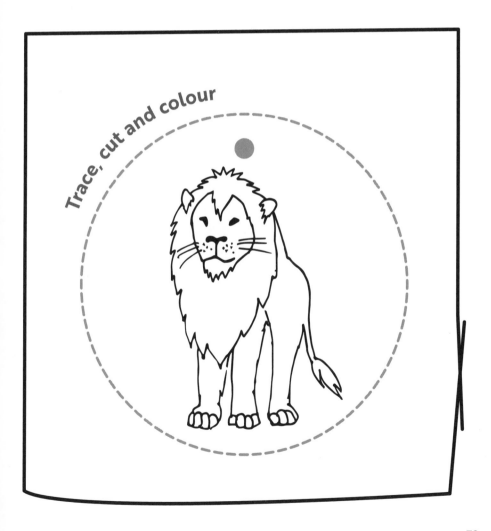

Trace, cut and colour

The place promised

Micah 5:2–5

'The LORD says, "Bethlehem Ephrathah, you are one of the smallest towns in Judah, but out of you I will bring a ruler for Israel, whose family line goes back to ancient times."

So the LORD will abandon his people to their enemies until the woman who is to give birth has her son. Then those Israelites who are in exile will be reunited with their own people. When he comes, he will rule his people with the strength that comes from the LORD and with the majesty of the LORD God himself. His people will live in safety because people all over the earth will acknowledge his greatness, and he will bring peace.'

Something to think about

Micah was another of God's prophets, carrying a message straight from God to His people. A lot of prophecies are like promises. This one certainly was. It came at a time when things were tough in Israel and enemies were planning to attack and take over. God was promising His people that although times were going to be tough, He would send a king who would change everything and bring peace. God's promises always come true – although not always quickly. But Israel knew that God was true to His word, so this promise brought them hope.

Pointing to Jesus

This promise says that God will bring a ruler out of Bethlehem, and we know that centuries later that's exactly where Jesus was born when Mary and Joseph had to go there for a government census. God kept every part of His promise, right down to the last detail. And we have been given a similar promise: Jesus is going to come again and bring a peace that will last forever.

Bekah says...

Knowing that God always keeps His promises is amazing. So many people don't, and it's often hard to know who to trust. Steve and I have taught our girls to be very careful about what they promise and to only say 'I promise...' if they're sure they mean it.

Christmas unwrapped

Some people don't like 'Xmas' being used as a substitute for 'Christmas' because they think that it's taking 'Christ' out of Christmas. But funnily enough, nothing could be further from the truth. 'Xmas' actually keeps Christ at the forefront because the Greek letter 'X' represents the 'Christ', and is said to have been around for 600 years. 'Christ' means Messiah or Anointed One. The 'mas' part comes from the word 'mass' – it's sometimes called Communion or Eucharist – where Christians remember when Jesus came back to life, that very first Easter.

Something to talk about

· What's the biggest promise you have ever made?
· How does it feel when someone breaks a promise?

Pray

Dear Jesus, thank You for being the Prince of peace. You are a good and loving King and I'm looking forward to the day You come to bring peace for good. On the days when it feels like my world is in trouble, help me to look to You to find my peace.
Amen.

Jesse tree

Today we're hanging a picture of Bethlehem on our tree to remind us that God keeps His promises and always has a plan.

Trace, cut and colour

Silence

Luke 1:5,7,11–13,15–17,18–20

'During the time when Herod was king of Judea, there was a priest named Zechariah... His wife's name was Elizabeth... They had no children because Elizabeth could not have any, and she and Zechariah were both very old...

An angel of the Lord appeared to [Zechariah], standing at the right side of the altar where the incense was burned. When Zechariah saw him, he was alarmed and felt afraid. But the angel said to him, "Don't be afraid, Zechariah! God has heard your prayer, and your wife Elizabeth will bear you a son. You are to name him John... he will be filled with the Holy Spirit, and he will bring back many of the people of Israel to the Lord their God. He will go ahead of the Lord..."

Zechariah said to the angel, "How shall I know if this is so? I am an old man, and my wife is old also."

"I am Gabriel," the angel answered. "I stand in the presence of God, who sent me to speak to you and tell you this good news. But you have not believed my message, which will come true at the right time. Because you have not believed, you will be unable to speak; you will remain silent until the day my promise to you comes true."'

Something to think about

Poor old Zechariah had a very long time of silence. It seems a bit harsh for not believing the angel who told him that he and his wife were going to have a baby in their old age, but perhaps it was really a gift? It certainly would have helped him to know for sure that he had met an angel, that he wasn't going mad and that he could believe the promise. It would also have given him a lot of time to think about all that had happened, everything he knew about God and what might be coming next.

Pointing to Jesus

Zechariah would soon be a relative of Jesus. In fact, it would only be a few months before Elizabeth's cousin Mary would have her own visit from an angel to tell her about a baby. Zechariah and Elizabeth's son was called John and he had a special mission: to prepare the way for Mary's son, Jesus. He was a bit like a doorbell, letting everyone know that Jesus was coming and giving everyone a chance to prepare their hearts to meet Him.

Bekah says...

I find being quiet very difficult! I love to talk. Sometimes it feels like I have so much happening in my head that I might burst if I don't let it out. But I have learned that if I don't stop talking, it's hard to listen, both to my family and to God.

Christmas unwrapped

Zechariah may have been quiet, but have you ever heard how loud turkeys are?! Cooked turkey might be a key part of your Christmas Day, but turkey wasn't eaten much before the sixteenth century. Before then the well-off would have eaten goose, boar's head or even a peacock! Turkeys originated from Mexico – not Turkey – and they were first imported from the USA to Europe, reaching the UK in 1525.

Something to talk about

· How easy do you find it to be quiet?
· Who in your family is a good listener?

Pray

Dear Father God, thank You for wanting to talk to me. Help me to be quiet long enough to hear what You have to say. Amen.

Jesse tree

Today we're hanging some praying hands on the tree to show us that it's good to sit still and be quiet sometimes to listen to God, just like Zechariah had to.

Trace, cut and colour

DAY 21

A new normal

Luke 1:26–35,38

'In the sixth month of Elizabeth's pregnancy God sent the angel Gabriel to a town in Galilee named Nazareth. He had a message for a young woman promised in marriage to a man named Joseph, who was a descendant of King David. Her name was Mary. The angel came to her and said, "Peace be with you! The Lord is with you and has greatly blessed you!"

Mary was deeply troubled by the angel's message, and she wondered what his words meant. The angel said to her, "Don't be afraid, Mary; God has been gracious to you. You will become pregnant and give birth to a son, and you will name him Jesus. He will be great and will be called the Son of the Most High God. The Lord God will make him a king, as his ancestor David was, and he will be the king of the descendants of Jacob forever; his kingdom will never end!"

Mary said to the angel, "I am a virgin. How, then, can this be?"

The angel answered, "The Holy Spirit will come on you, and God's power will rest upon you. For this reason the holy child will be called the Son of God."...

"I am the Lord's servant," said Mary; "may it happen to me as you have said." And the angel left her.'

Something to think about

After all the waiting, the time has finally come for God to fulfil all His promises. It feels like there should be a drum roll, or an amazing backing song like there would be in a film, or even a great spotlight from heaven as the announcement is made that the promised King is about to arrive. Instead we have a very ordinary teenage girl going about her very ordinary day, getting a very extraordinary visit from an angel. Nothing would ever be ordinary for Mary again. She might still have to do all the everyday things that mums do, but her life would change forever.

Pointing to Jesus

Jesus is finally coming. Following years of waiting and longing, the Prince of peace is on His way to save the world and make all things new.

Bekah says...

It's easy to miss how crazy this was for Mary. She would only have been about 13 or 14, and being pregnant could have got her in a lot of trouble. But Mary trusted God in a way that Zechariah didn't. She wants to serve God, no matter what that means. Her response isn't, 'No way!' (although that would have been understandable). Her answer is, 'I am Your servant.' What an awesome young woman she was. Perfect to be the mother of God's child.

Christmas unwrapped

In school nativity plays, children chosen to be angels often wear a long white dress and have some shiny wings and a head-band with a halo sticking up the top. But that's not what the Bible tells us about what angels look like. There are times when it describes angels as being dressed in white or shining, but there's no mention of wings at all.

Something to talk about

· Have you ever had to do something difficult for God?
· What happened?

Pray

Dear Jesus, thank You for choosing to become a human being, and being a baby in an ordinary young woman's tummy. Thank You for doing all this to save the world. Amen.

Jesse tree

Today we're putting a picture of Mary on the tree to help us remember how brave she was with her 'yes' to God. It will remind us try to be brave like her.

Trace, cut and colour

DAY 22

Do not be afraid

Matthew 1:18–25

'This was how the birth of Jesus Christ took place. His mother Mary was engaged to Joseph, but before they were married, she found out that she was going to have a baby by the Holy Spirit. Joseph was a man who always did what was right, but he did not want to disgrace Mary publicly; so he made plans to break the engagement privately. While he was thinking about this, an angel of the Lord appeared to him in a dream and said, "Joseph, descendant of David, do not be afraid to take Mary to be your wife. For it is by the Holy Spirit that she has conceived. She will have a son, and you will name him Jesus—because he will save his people from their sins."

Now all this happened in order to make come true what the Lord had said through the prophet, "A virgin will become pregnant and have a son, and he will be called Immanuel" (which means, "God is with us").

So when Joseph woke up, he married Mary, as the angel of the Lord had told him to. But he had no sexual relations with her before she gave birth to her son. And Joseph named him Jesus.'

Something to think about

Joseph had a tough decision to make. Mary's story must have seemed bonkers. It looked like she'd broken all the rules and was having someone else's baby, which would have been deeply embarrassing for him. But he valued Mary's life more than his pride, so he chose to discreetly break off the engagement. But after his own visit from an angel in a dream, he still had a tough decision to make. Would he set all his dreams for the future aside to support Mary with her amazing mission, or would he walk away? He chose to stay. Joseph is one of the most amazing men in the Bible. He chose to put God and his wife first and because of that got to be a dad to God's Son.

Pointing to Jesus

Joseph had to choose to be part of Jesus' story and it's the same for us. You won't have a toddler Jesus running around your house like Joseph did, but you still get to choose whether to follow Him and allow Him to be part of your life. What have you decided?

Bekah says...

I think it's amazing that Joseph got to teach Jesus how to use a hammer and build a table. But even greater than that is the fact that he would have taught Jesus to read the Bible and he certainly modelled how to love people well. What a fantastic privilege.

Christmas unwrapped

You may or may not be dreaming of snow this Christmas, but Irving Berlin certainly was when he wrote the song *White Christmas*. The version sung by Bing Crosby was released in 1942 and and became one of the best-selling records of all time.

Something to talk about

· What things have you learned from your parents?
· What would you love your children to learn from you?

Pray

Father God, thank You for inviting me to be part of Your story. Please show me if there are areas of my life where I'm more bothered about what people think of me than following You. Amen.

Jesse tree

Today we're hanging an angel on the tree to remind us that God has a plan for us to be part of His story too if we choose to follow Him.

Trace, cut and colour

A long journey

Luke 2:1–6

'At that time Emperor Augustus ordered a census to be taken throughout the Roman Empire. When this first census took place, Quirinius was the governor of Syria. Everyone, then, went to register himself, each to his own hometown.

Joseph went from the town of Nazareth in Galilee to the town of Bethlehem in Judea, the birthplace of King David. Joseph went there because he was a descendant of David. He went to register with Mary, who was promised in marriage to him. She was pregnant, and while they were in Bethlehem, the time came for her to have her baby.'

Something to think about

We've travelled quite far through the Bible this Advent, preparing for the arrival of Jesus – and He's nearly here. Now we're on our way to Bethlehem, the town that was prophesied as the birthplace of the new King. Mary, about to give birth, must be big and uncomfortable and desperate to see her new child. Joseph is probably desperately hoping he'll find somewhere for his family that is safe, desperately hoping the baby won't come too soon and desperately hoping he'll be a good enough dad for the Son of God. Can you imagine the anticipation? We all get excited waiting for Christmas, but Joseph and Mary must have been bursting to see what would happen.

Pointing to Jesus

What are you looking forward to this Christmas? Presents? Food? Visitors? In the midst of all that, it's easy to forget how exciting it is that Jesus came to earth as a baby. Take some time to really appreciate what it means that God came down to earth.

Bekah says...

I can sympathise with Mary. My first child was late arriving and I had such a big tummy, I could hardly put my own shoes on! I was desperate to see my baby, to find out if it was a boy or a girl, to see what colour eyes she had and to give her a big cuddle and a kiss. I get a bit emotional just thinking about it. But I can't imagine how much more intense it must have been to wait for Jesus to be born.

Christmas unwrapped

What do Isaac Newton, Chris Kamara, Annie Lennox and Jesus all have in common? They were all born on Christmas Day – well, except Jesus that is! The Romans first celebrated 25 December as the birth of Christ in AD 336, when the emperor became a Christian and announced that a pagan festival celebrating the power of the sun would now be a celebration of the Son of God.

Something to talk about

- When have you had something exciting to look forward to?
- How did you feel during the waiting?

Pray

Jesus, we're so excited about Christmas and all the fun we will have. But we choose to stop for a while and think about how exciting is that You arrived all those years ago, and look forward to the day when You will come again. Thank You so much. Amen.

Jesse tree

Let's hang some sandals on the tree today to remind us of the long journey that Mary and Joseph went on.

Trace, cut and colour

A big announcement

Luke 2:8–14,17–20

'There were some shepherds in that part of the country who were spending the night in the fields, taking care of their flocks. An angel of the Lord appeared to them, and the glory of the Lord shone over them. They were terribly afraid, but the angel said to them, "Don't be afraid! I am here with good news for you, which will bring great joy to all the people. This very day in David's town your Saviour was born—Christ the Lord! And this is what will prove it to you: you will find a baby wrapped in cloths and lying in a manger."

Suddenly a great army of heaven's angels appeared with the angel, singing praises to God:

"Glory to God in the highest heaven,
and peace on earth to those with whom he is pleased!"...

When the shepherds saw [the baby], they told [Mary and Joseph] what the angel had said about the child. All who heard it were amazed at what the shepherds said. Mary remembered all these things and thought deeply about them. The shepherds went back, singing praises to God for all they had heard and seen; it had been just as the angel had told them.'

Something to think about

He's here! After all the clues and hints and signposts, in the darkness of a smelly stable, a child is born. A light shines in the darkness and finally, from the stump of the tree of Jesse, a shoot breaks through. Jesus is here. The waiting is over, hope has arrived, the promise has been kept. Tomorrow, on Christmas Day, we'll all celebrate this amazing day.

Mary is holding her precious baby boy and wondering how this little bundle will grow up to change the world. Joseph is watching over them both, the proud father of a healthy boy. The angels are celebrating, proclaiming the news, unable to contain their joy as they praise their God in heaven.

Out on the hills, the shepherds are the first to hear the news and make their way to visit the baby. They're not seen as particularly important people, in fact they were quite the opposite, but they are given the first invitation to meet the shepherd King. And they can't keep the news to themselves – they tell everyone that they have met the Saviour of the world.

You can be like one of those shepherds. It doesn't matter who you are, you are invited to meet Jesus, to come and spend time with Him, and then to go and tell the good news to everyone you know.

Bekah says...

I love that God chooses the unexpected people to be part of His story and asks them to share the greatest news the world has ever had. We live in a world where people care way too much about being famous and seen as important. Jesus doesn't care about any of that. He loves everyone and so often uses the least 'important' people for the most important jobs. That's pretty exciting.

Christmas unwrapped

Just before Jesus was born, an angel appeared to Joseph and instructed him to call his son Jesus, 'because he will save his people from their sins' (Matt. 1:21, NIV). Jesus came to take away the guilt and punishment that our wrong thoughts, words and actions deserve, and to bring us to God. He made a way for forgiveness, and the good news is that it's still available today. It's a wonderful gift – It's there if you want it. Whoever you are, wherever you are, Jesus is for you.

Something to talk about

· What's the best news you've ever heard?
· Who did you tell about it?

Pray

Jesus, You came! We're so glad. Thank You so much for leaving heaven and coming to be born to save the world. We love You. Amen.

Jesse tree

Today we can hang a picture of baby Jesus on our tree because we're celebrating that after all the waiting He is finally here!

Trace, cut and colour

Other books to help you journey together...

Take time out each day to encounter the God who created you, loves you and has plans for each of you! Over 12 weeks discover more about what it means to follow God, as Steve and Bekah Legg bring a fun, engaging and personal approach to reading the Bible.

❝ A great resource to bring the family together to talk about the things that matter. ❞
Rob Parsons

To find out more and to order, visit **cwr.org.uk/thefamilydevotional** or call **01252 784700**.

Also available in Christian bookshops.

Connecting with God, your family and others

Find God in your Every Day...

There's something for everyone!

Ten minutes with God every day can change your life.

Spend time seeking God's voice every day and see how your own faith deepens and grows, or encourage a friend or family member with a one-year gift subscription.

cwr.org.uk/brn

Waverley Abbey College

Courses and seminars

Publishing and media

Conference facilities

Transforming lives

CWR's vision is to enable people to experience personal transformation through applying God's Word to their lives and relationships.

Our Bible-based training and resources help people around the world to:
- Grow in their walk with God
- Understand and apply Scripture to their lives
- Resource themselves and their church
- Develop pastoral care and counselling skills
- Train for leadership
- Strengthen relationships, marriage and family life and much more.

Our insightful writers provide daily Bible reading notes and other resources for all ages, and our experienced course designers and presenters have gained an international reputation for excellence and effectiveness.

CWR's Training and Conference Centre in Surrey, England, provides excellent facilities in an idyllic setting – ideal for both learning and spiritual refreshment.

CWR Applying God's Word
to everyday life and relationships

CWR, Waverley Abbey House,
Waverley Lane, Farnham,
Surrey GU9 8EP, UK

Telephone: **+44 (0)1252 784700**
Email: **info@cwr.org.uk**
Website: **www.cwr.org.uk**

Registered Charity No. 294387
Company Registration No. 1990308